RISE WITH JESUS:
30 DAYS TO TRANSFORM YOUR LIFE

The Prayer

BY STEFANIA FERNANDA LEAO &
ALEXANDER DEBELOV

Copyright © 2025 by Stefania Fernanda Leao & Alexander Debelov

All rights reserved.

No portion of this book may be reproduced in any form without written permission from the publisher or author, except as permitted by U.S. copyright law.

Introduction

For a long time, I've carried the desire to create a book that connects the daily challenges we face with the timeless truths of God's Word. Many people struggle to make prayer and meditation on Scripture a daily habit, even though the difficulties of life never pause. Every day, we're exposed to advice and words that can discourage or even harm our spirit. That's why it's crucial to let the Holy Spirit guide us, helping us resist being captive to negativity.

The choice of what words will shape your life is yours alone. This book is designed to help you integrate prayer and meditation on God's Word into any moment of your day. With the remarkable illustrations of Alexander Debelov bringing these pages to life, we've crafted a journey that's as visually inspiring as it is spiritually enriching. I encourage you to reflect on the verses, make notes, and track your spiritual journey as you go. Perseverance in faith comes from consistency in reading and living out God's Word. Remember, change happens not just by reading the Bible but by practicing its teachings.

My prayer is that this book will help you discover God's promises for your life and experience the depth of His love. May it be a blessing to you, in Jesus' name.

Stefania Fernanda Leao & Alex Debelov

Day 1: Time To Be Blessed

Psalm 91:9-10

Because you, Lord, are my refuge. You have made the Most High your dwelling place. No harm will overtake you; no plague will come near your tent.

Reflection:

Begin this day in God's presence. Everything that starts well ends well. Take refuge in Him and trust His promise, for He does not lie! The certainty that you are safe is what we call conscious faith. It is this faith that sustains you during the hardest days, keeping you steady and confident no matter what happens, knowing you are secure.

Prayer:

Lord Jesus, I choose to dwell in the shelter of the Most High. I declare that this is my time to be blessed, healed, and set free. Look upon my troubles, and grant me Your peace and security. I pray this in the name of Jesus. Amen.

Day 2: Trust in Lord's Love

PSALM 40:1

I waited patiently for the LORD; He turned to me and heard my cry for help.

Reflection:

Trust is what brings peace when we are waiting for an answer. It's the courage we need to live by faith. There is no such thing as trusting while doubting. Why is it easier to trust in people than in God? People can fail you, but God never will. No matter how hard your day may be, trust in the Lord, and He will hear your cry.

Prayer:

Lord Jesus, I choose to trust in You. Sustain me until victory comes. You are the strength of my life, and Your favor is upon me. Rescue me from destruction, restore me, and help me live by Your Word. Teach me to trust in Your love. My covenant with You is one of life and peace, and I freely receive from the source of life. Thank You for loving me so much. This is my prayer and gratitude. Amen.

Day 3: Be a Source of Love

LUKE 6:45

A good man brings good things out of the good stored up in his heart, and an evil man brings evil things out of the evil stored up in his heart. For the mouth speaks what the heart is full of.

Reflection:

Be mindful of what comes out of your mouth—words have the power to bless or curse. What you say can produce life or death. When you speak words of life to someone, they also bless you; when you speak words of defeat or harm, they come back to you as well. What have your lips honored more—darkness or light? Speak words like: I believe, I can, I will not fear, I will keep going until I succeed. Your life reflects the words you confess.

Prayer:

Lord Jesus, help me to speak words that will be a blessing to my life and to those around me. The fear of the Lord brings health to my body and strength to my bones. I declare that from today onward, my mouth will be a source of life, love, joy, peace, healing, and encouragement. Amen.

Day 4: Exercise Your Faith

JOHN 16:33

"I have told you these things, so that in me you may have peace. In this world you will have trouble. But take heart! I have overcome the world."

Reflection:

The Lord Jesus assures us of His peace and presence, but He never promised a life without struggles. The battles we face are opportunities to strengthen our faith. In this world, we will encounter problems and afflictions, but Jesus makes it clear that if we walk with Him, we too will overcome. Without battles, there can be no victories, and only those who fight—those who refuse to give in to problems or settle for less—can truly win. Don't let your faith become stagnant.

Prayer:

Lord Jesus, I declare that every problem I face is an opportunity to exercise my faith and overcome. I trust that wisdom and knowledge are my stability in this season, and You are the strength of my salvation. The fear of the Lord is my treasure. I declare that from now on, Your divine wisdom will bring me success, and my heart will guide me to make the right choices because I am wise in Christ. Amen.

Day 5: A Present Help

Psalm 46:11

The Lord Almighty is with us; the God of Jacob is our refuge.

Reflection:

If God is your refuge and strength, there's no need to fear—even the worst problems. When your life is grounded in Him, and He is your shelter, you are protected. Even if the earth shifts or the mountains crumble, even if the waters rage, the Holy Spirit is at work, bringing you peace and security. God promises to be with us, and it's up to us to obey His command: Be still and know that I am God. Anxiety is like a rocking chair—it keeps you moving but doesn't get you anywhere.

Prayer:

Jesus, help me calm my heart so I can believe that You are with me. I trust You as my help and my protection. I humble myself before You, Lord. I pray and seek Your face, turning away from all wrong paths, knowing that You will hear my prayers from heaven. You will forgive my sins and bring me Your healing. Amen.

Day 6: Renewed Strength

Isaiah 40:31

But those who hope in the Lord will renew their strength. They will soar on wings like eagles; they will run and not grow weary, they will walk and not be faint.

Reflection:

It's natural to feel tired—not just from physical activity but also from the daily struggles and battles we face. Yet, God never grows tired, and He will not stop fighting for us. He promises to multiply our strength. In God, strength is renewed regardless of age. If you're feeling weary, remember this promise: strength doesn't come from your muscles, your age, or even your health—it comes from the Holy Spirit. Today, you can receive what has already been promised: renewed strength.

Prayer:

Lord, renew my strength like the eagle's. Multiply my strength here on earth. I will not forget Your benefits, for You have forgiven my sins and healed all my diseases. You have redeemed my life from destruction and crowned me with mercy! I declare that Your hand will sustain me every second of my life, and I surrender my heart at Your altar. Amen.

Day 7: The Harvest

GALATIANS 6:9

Let us not become weary in doing good, for at the proper time we will reap a harvest if we do not give up.

Reflection:

Our personal needs often shift our focus inward—we tend to fixate on our problems, our lives, and our worries about the future. This can pull our hearts and attention away from generosity. Don't grow tired of doing good, whether you are appreciated or not, understood or not. If you want to prosper, be generous. If you want your thirst quenched, offer someone a drink. If you want love, give love. If you want attention, give attention. You cannot receive what you do not give—it's a divine law. Nature works this way: you reap what you sow.

Prayer:

Lord, I will plant what I want to harvest from now on. Teach me to serve, to heal, to love, to respect, and to be generous. Help me see others through Your eyes and fulfill Your commandments so that, through Your Word, I may be blessed in the name of Your beloved Son, Jesus Christ. Amen.

Day 8: Let Go of the Weights

HEBREWS 12:1

Therefore, since we are surrounded by such a great cloud of witnesses, let us throw off everything that hinders and the sin that so easily entangles. And let us run with perseverance the race marked out for us.

Reflection:

Do yourself a favor: let go of old burdens that bring doubt and won't lead you anywhere. Examples include unfulfilled promises, resentment, insecurity, fear, malice, or mistrust. Free yourself from these weights—they only slow down your journey. Ask God for forgiveness for unkept promises, rash decisions, and words you couldn't keep. You cannot allow the enemy or your conscience to accuse you any longer. Forgive others and forgive yourself. A lack of forgiveness is an anchor that keeps you stuck.

Prayer:

Lord Jesus, I use the shield of faith to extinguish all the flaming arrows the enemy sends my way. I choose to break free from all curses of a wandering and aimless life. I break free from every negative word spoken over me by others, and from all the negativity I've spoken over myself. I release forgiveness and forgive myself. I declare that I am blessed and free from all burdens, in the name of Jesus! Amen.

Day 9: Unconditional Love

For God so loved the world that He gave His one and only Son, that whoever believes in Him shall not perish but have eternal life.

Reflection:

Jesus is the bread of life; only He can satisfy our thirst for love! What is this world that God loved so much? What did He love, and how much does He love us? The "world" is us—He loved us so deeply, intensely, and incomparably that He gave His only Son to die on the cross for our sins. The crucifixion of Jesus is the greatest demonstration of love. Jesus was sent in His entirety for us, out of love, to give us the chance to be forgiven and to live fully as children of God, because the essence of God is fatherhood.

Prayer:

Lord Jesus, I declare that from now on, I will no longer say I was never loved, because true love was shown to me through Jesus on the cross at Calvary. I declare that I am loved and carry the essence of Christ, and I reject all insecurity, fear, and the need for validation. I accept Christ's love over me and surrender completely to it. I feel eternally loved, and nothing and no one will make me feel otherwise. I forgive all those who, for any reason, abandoned me or made me feel unloved. I am loved—even if my earthly father failed to fulfill his role. I am no longer bound by past feelings, because Christ's love heals me now, in Jesus' name. Amen.

Day 10: Faith and Prayer

Hebrews 11:6

And without faith it is impossible to please God, because anyone who comes to Him must believe that He exists and that He rewards those who earnestly seek Him.

Reflection:

What pleases God's heart is faith. Prayer is the only path that allows us to know Him in the deepest truth. Love requires relationship, and this is the foundation of our connection with the Lord. We have duties and responsibilities toward God's Word, but we also have rights and privileges to His promises.

Prayer:

Lord Jesus, I declare that from now on, my faith will be grounded in You. I place my trust under the shadow of Your wings, where I will be abundantly satisfied with the fullness of Your house. In You is a fountain of life. I believe that faith means trusting in the incredible, seeing the invisible, and receiving the impossible. Amen.

Day 11: It's Already Done

NEHEMIAH 6:9

They were all trying to frighten us, thinking, "Their hands will get too weak for the work, and it will not be completed." But I prayed, "Now strengthen my hands."

Reflection:

Have you noticed how often, when you set out to accomplish something, there are always people saying it won't work, that you can't do it, or that it won't succeed? They aim to make you stop halfway through. Don't let those words of defeat settle in your heart. Don't listen to attempts to intimidate you. God is in control of your life.

Prayer:

Lord Jesus, I ask You to strengthen my hands and my heart. Remove every obstacle from my path and help me move forward to finish what I've started. It's a matter of honor, and I will succeed because You are with me. I declare that my only option is to win. I won't leave until I've completed what needs to be done. Be my guide, Jesus. Amen.

Day 12: The Perfect Timing

HABAKKUK 2:3

For the revelation awaits an appointed time; it speaks of the end and will not prove false. Though it linger, wait for it; it will certainly come and will not delay.

Reflection:

This verse is a promise from God to you. Waiting is not vague hope; it is a confident expectation. A pregnant woman must wait nine months to give birth. Why are we often in such a rush? Rushing leads to wrong decisions and careless words. The enemy, knowing our needs, uses anxiety to sow doubt in our hearts—questions like "When will it happen?" or "Why is it taking so long?" These doubts weaken our faith. Never forget: God's timing is perfect.

Prayer:

Lord Jesus, I know Your timing is perfect. Fulfill Your plans for my life, and help me not to be anxious. I trust that everything happens neither too early nor too late, because You are perfect in all You do. I declare that I will not let anxiety take hold of me. I will be happy and live out Your plans in the right season You have already prepared for me. From now on, I won't lose sleep, my smile, or my joy because of things that haven't yet arrived. Amen.

Day 13: Self-Control

Ephesians 4:26-27

"In your anger do not sin": Do not let the sun go down while you are still angry, and do not give the devil a foothold.

Reflection:

It's natural to feel anger at times—God understands this. However, it's essential to have the wisdom not to let this feeling grow and take root within us. The heart often wants to fight, hurt, offend, or seek revenge, but reason helps us resist those urges and prevents anger from consuming us. Make the right choice: forgive, repent, and stay vigilant. Close the doors that lead to wounding others or being wounded yourself.

Prayer:

Lord Jesus, I declare that this is my time to be healed. I repent of my iniquities and pray that You forgive the thoughts of my heart. I don't want to be trapped by bitterness, unforgiveness, revenge, anger, or rage. From now on, I will forgive those who need to be forgiven, and I also ask for forgiveness for the times I have hurt others (you may name them if you wish) and grieved Your heart. Help me to be healed so that I can bring healing to others, rather than harm. I will take control of my emotions and not let them control me. Amen.

Day 14: A New Story

Isaiah 43:18-19

"Forget the former things; do not dwell on the past. See, I am doing a new thing! Now it springs up; do you not perceive it? I am making a way in the wilderness and streams in the wasteland."

Reflection:

The time for God's newness has arrived in your life! The struggles you've been enduring have a purpose: to lead you into Jesus' arms. In this season of new beginnings, the past should only serve as a reminder to propel you toward the future God has already designed. Memories that don't help you will only hinder you; if they don't lift you up, they'll pull you down. If they don't make you grow, leave them behind. Do not walk under a verdict that isn't from God.

Prayer:

Father, in the name of Jesus, I release myself from the effects of all painful memories and past experiences that keep me from living fully in the present and embracing the future. Circumstances will not steal what You have given me, and I declare that the season of Your newness has come to my life. Amen.

Day 15: The Price of Conquest

EXODUS 3:19

"But I know that the king of Egypt will not let you go unless a mighty hand compels him."

Reflection:

The greater the victory, the tougher the battle and the bigger the sacrifice. The liberation of the Hebrews from Pharaoh seemed impossible. Pharaoh thrived on the enslavement of the people, making their freedom appear out of reach. Yet God demonstrated His greatness and mercy by raising up Moses to deliver them. The battle was not fought with swords or physical strength but through heaven moving on behalf of His people, rendering Pharaoh powerless. This is why faith is certainty, conviction, and assurance. Achieving something significant in this world requires sacrifice, courage, effort, hard work, and unshakable faith.

Prayer:

Father, in the name of Jesus, I understand that faith demands firmness, certainty, and conviction. Evil will not yield unless compelled by a mighty hand, and that hand is Yours, Lord. I declare that from this moment on, nothing that has bound me will hold me any longer. Everything that sought to hinder my path will be stopped in its tracks. Your mighty hand moves against my adversaries. Lord, part the Red Sea in my life so I may walk through and experience transformation and freedom in Your presence. Whatever or whoever symbolizes Pharaoh in my life will no longer have power over me or any area of my life. I pray and believe this in the mighty name of Jesus. Amen.

Day 16: Opportunities in Christ

Psalm 69:1

"Save me, O God, for the waters have come up to my neck."

Reflection:

David faced relentless battles with his enemies, and many of the Psalms reflect his moments of deep anguish. One profound lesson we learn is that our times of pain are also the greatest opportunities to activate and strengthen our faith. These moments keep us anchored in God, ensuring that we don't grow complacent or risk losing sight of His promises. The greater the battle, the stronger our faith and dependence on God must be. Spiritual health thrives under the challenges that bring us closer to Him.

Prayer:

Father, in the name of Jesus, protect me from every kind of evil. Sanctify me through the truth of Your Word and strengthen my faith deep within me by Your power. Let me know the true love of Christ, and grant me patience, self-control, and joy. May my faith never falter. I rebuke, in Jesus' name, all spiritual coldness, mental weakness, and psychological confusion. I decree that my faith will always remain firmly rooted in the Lord Jesus Christ. So be it, Amen.

Day 17: Idle Conversations

1 CORINTHIANS 15:33

"Do not be deceived: 'Bad company corrupts good character."

Reflection:

Keep your distance from gossips, negative people, speculators, and the overly curious. These individuals spread information recklessly, often without regard for the truth or the harm they cause. They can tarnish reputations and are not to be trusted. Guard the purity of your faith and heart by choosing your associations wisely. Cultivate intimacy with the Holy Spirit and practice discernment when judging the information you hear. Remember, if you sit and entertain idle talk today, your life could be the subject of it tomorrow. Protect your character by avoiding unproductive and harmful conversations.

Prayer:

Father, in the name of Jesus, grant me wisdom to choose my friends and confidants carefully. Deliver me from idle and harmful conversations that can corrupt the good within me. I declare in the name of Jesus that every spirit of gossip, confusion, disturbance, and negativity will stay far from my life, my thoughts, my heart, and my lips. I commit to maintaining integrity in my words and actions, trusting in Your guidance. Amen.

Day 18: You Are Valuable

1 Corinthians 7:23

"You were bought at a price; do not become slaves of men."

Reflection:

You are precious to God. The greatest demonstration of love was Jesus giving His life on the cross for you and me. Don't entrust your life to those who cannot truly help you. Refuse to settle for crumbs or accept less than what you deserve. Small mistakes can cause significant doubts, and those doubts can lead to deep wounds in your soul. In Christ, you are free. His blood was the price paid to deliver you from the slavery of sin and grant you the honor of becoming a king and priest for God. Your freedom has been purchased, and in Him, you are clean and redeemed. Remember, when you settle for less, you lose the right to complain about the outcome.

Prayer:

Jesus, deliver me from evil and preserve me from those who seek to harm me. Guard me, O Lord, from the hands of the wicked and do not let the plans of the enemy succeed in my life. Thank You, Jesus, for Your care and protection. I surrender my life to You, declaring that You are my only Savior and the Lord of my life. In Your holy name, I pray. Amen.

Day 19: Do Your Part

MATTHEW 9:6

"But so that you may know that the Son of Man has authority on earth to forgive sins"—then He said to the paralyzed man—"Get up, take your mat, and go home."

Reflection:

It is challenging to enjoy the fullness of life and then settle for its crumbs. This is how it feels for those who have experienced the joy of salvation but, for some reason, returned to the world and lost spiritual values. Jesus' command is clear: to rise and walk. Prayer alone does not force someone to stand up—it requires personal action through obedience.

Faith must not be passive or stagnant; it requires movement and commitment. Don't grow complacent in your spiritual walk.

Prayer:

Father, in the name of Jesus, I declare that from this moment on, I will not grow complacent in my faith. I will walk under Your grace and follow Your commands. Teach me to seek integrity, for Your Word says that the integrity of the righteous will guide them. Help me to rise, obey, and act in accordance with Your will. In Jesus' name, I pray. Amen.

Day 20: Strength in Weakness

2 CORINTHIANS 12:9

"My grace is sufficient for you, for my power is made perfect in weakness."

Reflection:

God's power shines brightest in our moments of weakness. When we feel incapable, He steps in with His sufficient grace, teaching us that our strength doesn't come from our abilities but from His presence in us. Instead of being overwhelmed by our limitations, we should trust in His limitless strength and rely on Him fully.

THE PRAYER

Prayer:

Lord, I acknowledge my weaknesses before You. Help me to trust in Your power and grace to sustain me. Thank You for working through my struggles to show Your greatness. I declare that my strength comes from You, and I will not be shaken by my limitations. In Jesus' name, Amen.

Day 21: Trust in God's Timing

ECCLESIASTES 3:11

"He has made everything beautiful in its time."

Reflection:

Impatience can rob us of peace, especially when we long for things to happen on our schedule. Yet, God's timing is perfect, and His plans are beau-tiful. Trusting Him means surrendering our need for control and believing that His purpose for us will come to fruition at the right moment.

Prayer:

Father, help me to trust Your timing and plans for my life. Teach me patience and help me to rest in Your promises, knowing that You are working all things for my good. In Jesus' name, Amen.

Day 22: The Power of Words

Psalm 19:14

"Let the words of my mouth and the meditation of my heart be acceptable in Your sight, O Lord, my strength and my Redeemer."

Reflection:

Our words hold power to build up or tear down. What we speak reflects what is in our hearts. By surrendering our speech to God, we allow Him to guide our words to bring life and encouragement to others. Speak blessings, not curses, and allow your heart to remain focused on what is good.

Prayer:

Lord, I surrender my words to You. Help me to speak life, love, and encouragement to those around me. May my words always be pleasing in Your sight and reflect Your character. In Jesus' name, Amen.

Day 23: Light in Darkness

Psalm 27:1

"The Lord is my light and my salvation—whom shall I fear?"

Reflection:

Fear often thrives in darkness, but God is our eternal light. When we feel overwhelmed by uncertainty or challenges, we can remember that His presence illuminates our path. No matter how dark the situation seems, His light will always guide us and give us courage.

THE PRAYER

Prayer:

Lord, You are my light and salvation. I trust You to guide me through any darkness I face. Help me to walk in faith, knowing that Your light dispels all fear. In Jesus' name, Amen.

Day 24: A Heart of Gratitude

1 Thessalonians 5:18

"Give thanks in all circumstances; for this is God's will for you in Christ Jesus."

Reflection:

Gratitude shifts our perspective, even in difficult times. By choosing to give thanks, we acknowledge God's goodness and faithfulness in every situation. A thankful heart opens the door for joy and contentment, no matter what we face.

Prayer:

Lord, thank You for Your constant presence in my life. Help me to have a heart of gratitude and to see Your blessings, even in challenging circumstances. I give thanks to You for all things. In Jesus' name, Amen.

Day 25: Walking in Humility

James 4:10

"Humble yourselves before the Lord, and He will lift you up."

Reflection:

True humility is recognizing our dependence on God. When we humble ourselves, we allow Him to work in and through us. Pride builds walls, but humility invites God's grace and favor. Seek to walk humbly, trusting that God will exalt you in His time.

Prayer:

Father, I humble myself before You today. Teach me to depend on You in all things and to walk with a heart of humility. I trust You to lift me up in Your perfect timing. In Jesus' name, Amen.

Day 26: Peace Beyond Understanding

Philippians 4:7

"And the peace of God, which transcends all understanding, will guard your hearts and your minds in Christ Jesus."

Reflection:

The peace of God is not based on circumstances but on His presence in our lives. It surpasses human understanding and brings calm even in the midst of chaos. When we fix our minds on Him, His peace will guard our hearts and keep us secure.

Prayer:

Lord, I surrender my worries and fears to You. Fill me with Your peace that surpasses all understanding. Guard my heart and mind, and help me to rest in You. In Jesus' name, Amen.

Day 27: God's Provision

Philippians 4:19

"And my God will meet all your needs according to the riches of His glory in Christ Jesus."

Reflection:

God is a faithful provider. He knows our needs before we even ask and delights in supplying them. Trust in His provision and remember that He cares for you deeply. He is Jehovah Jireh, your Provider.

Prayer:

Father, thank you for being my Provider. I trust You to meet all my needs, both physical and spiritual. Help me to rely on Your faithfulness and not to worry about tomorrow. In Jesus' name, Amen.

Day 28: Forgiveness

EPHESIANS 4:32

"Be kind and compassionate to one another, forgiving each other, just as in Christ God forgave you."

Reflection:

Forgiveness is a gift we both give and receive. Just as Christ forgave us, we are called to forgive others. Holding onto bitterness only hurts us. Release those who have wronged you and experience the freedom that comes with forgiveness.

Prayer:

Lord, help me to forgive others as You have forgiven me. I release any bitterness or anger in my heart. Teach me to walk in kindness and compassion, reflecting Your love to those around me. In Jesus' name, Amen.

Day 29: Renewing Your Mind

ROMANS 12:2

"Do not conform to the pattern of this world, but be transformed by the renewing of your mind."

Reflection:

Our minds are powerful and need renewal daily through God's Word. Transformation begins with aligning our thoughts with His truth. Don't allow the world's patterns to shape you; instead, let God's Spirit mold your mind and character.

Prayer:

Lord, renew my mind and transform my thinking. Help me to focus on Your truth and not be swayed by the patterns of this world. I surrender my thoughts to You, trusting You to guide me. In Jesus' name, Amen.

Day 30: Faithful to the End

Matthew 25:23

"Well done, good and faithful servant!
You have been faithful with a few things;
I will put you in charge of many things."

Reflection:

God honors faithfulness, no matter how small the task. When we serve Him wholeheartedly, we bring glory to His name. Stay faithful in the little things, trusting that He sees your efforts and will reward your diligence.

Prayer:

Lord, help me to be faithful in all things, big and small. May I serve You with a joyful heart, knowing that You see my labor. I trust You to guide me and reward my faithfulness in Your time. In Jesus' name, Amen.

These additional pages complete your 30 reflections and prayers. Let me know if you need further assistance!

Final Thoughts: A Journey of Faith

As you turned the pages of this book, I hope you felt God's presence guiding each step of your journey. The walk of faith is filled with highs and lows, challenges and victories, but in all things, God remains faithful. He is the same yesterday, today, and forever, and His plans for you are greater than anything you could ever imagine.

Each reflection, each prayer written here was designed to encourage you, renew your hope, and remind you that you are never alone. When you pray, heaven moves on your behalf. When you trust, God acts. And when you obey, He manifests the supernatural in your life.

Never forget this: you are deeply loved by God. You are valuable, purposeful, and have a promise of eternal life in Christ Jesus. The road may not always be easy, but the Lord will be with you every step of the way—holding your hand, strengthening your heart, and showing you the path forward.

If I can leave you with one last encouragement, it is this: keep going. Keep believing, keep praying, keep seeking. No matter how difficult the moment may seem, remember that God is in control, and He will never leave nor forsake you.

May this book serve as a constant reminder of God's love and faithfulness. Return to these pages whenever you need comfort, inspiration, or direction.

My prayer is that you live out all that God has planned for you, that your faith grows stronger each day, and that you experience the fullness of life that Christ offers.

With faith and love,

Stefania Fernanda Leao & Alexander Debelov

www.ingramcontent.com/pod-product-compliance
Lightning Source LLC
Chambersburg PA
CBHW061342040426
42444CB00011B/3051